The Wild Side of Florida

A Children's Introduction to the Great Wildlife of Florida

By David Scardaville

Let's start our journey out on the water. It's better to follow a gator than be followed by one, so come and meet some of the wild animals of Florida...

STARFISH

Florida is a tropical state and is known most for its beaches. Our first stop on our adventure is Anastasia State park, in St. Augustine. These starfish stayed out to greet us. They are usually found near coral reefs, but today they're hanging beach-side so they must've known we were coming. Did you know a starfish isn't actually a fish? It is actually an echinoderm. Remember how the scarecrow used to say, "If I only had a brain?" Well, starfish do not have brains yet they seem to do OK without them.

BOTTLENOSE DOLPHIN

The Atlantic Beach was nice, but let's see what is in the Gulf Coast by taking our kayaks on the water near Anclote Key. Oh no! Is that a shark? I don't think so. It's likely a friendly dolphin. Dolphins are believed to have been land animals in ancient times and evolved to the point where they couldn't come back to land. Dolphins can get much more oxygen from the air then we can, so they can hold their breath much longer. But they can drown just like humans if they don't come up for air. Unlike most animals, dolphins have to think about breathing. Only half their brain sleeps at one time to keep breathing and a watchful eye for predators, so they actually sleep with one eye open.

EASTERN SQUIRREL

Florida wildlife isn't only found on the water, so let's go hiking in the Ocala National Forest! As we first hike into the woods we see a familiar looking animal. These squirrels can be found anywhere and everywhere, from your house to the forest. This particular tree mouse was very protective of his palm tree and did not want anyone to interfere. While you can find a squirrel anywhere, they generally live in trees. Often in homes built by woodpeckers, other times in the leaves. They give their nests away to their kids when the next litter is coming due.

GOPHER TORTOISE

Hey! He doesn't like being called a turtle! As we look down to the ground we see this gopher tortoise. While technically a type of turtle, you won't catch him swimming in any rivers or ponds. These half-shells live on land, often far from water. They are one of the oldest animal species still roaming the earth today; proving you can't keep a good shell down. They dig around 30-foot deep holes in the dirt where they live unlike any other... ah hum... half-shell. There are around 250 other species of animals that will use these burrows as homes when the tortoise decides to move, making them one of the homebuilders of the woods for many.

FLORIDA BLACK BEAR

Florida may not have any mountains, but it does have bears! It is the largest land animal living in Florida, but is a rare treat to find. They are very shy and secretive, living in very thick brush to remain hidden. They will mostly eat plants, and even honey, but are not too picky about what they eat in the "enchanted" Ocala Forest. They are an endangered species and there are only a few places big enough for them to live. It's best to keep a distance from these guys, and don't try to hide in a tree to escape them. Despite their size, they are excellent tree climbers.

FLORIDA SCRUB JAY

As we hike along we find a feathered tree dweller of the forest. Scrub jays are one of the endangered and protected species in Florida. These blue birds are very territorial. They have to be, there habitat is limited to sandy oak scrub areas which have been shrinking from buildings taking their place. By the way, you're not the only species that has chores! The Florida scrub jays stick together in small family groups. The children remain with the family as helpers in the tree-household for years. They move out when they are old enough to be moms and dads themselves.

PYGMY RATTLESNAKE

Don't keep your eyes in the trees too long. With cat-eyes and a venomous look, you may mistake this snake as a baby diamond back, but it is actually a fully grown pygmy rattler. This one is actually rather large for this species. They are usually less than 2 feet long. Don't let the size fool you though, they are just as dangerous as their bigger brothers and thought to be more likely to strike. Pygmy rattlers are the smallest venomous snakes in the USA. These snakes primarily use heat to find their prey, like infrared vision. When they strike their prey, they inject venom into them and allow them to run away. The animal will later die and the pygmy will track it by scent, or smelling where it went. A lot of people think the snake "rattles" its tail to scare you. It really does it to attract small animals which it wishes to eat.

AMERICAN ALLIGATOR

When thinking Florida, who doesn't picture an American Alligator? Our next paddling adventure brings us to Wekiwa River State Park where we found an example of Florida's best known mascot. Being in existence for over 150 Million years, these reptiles are the closest thing we have to a modern Dinosaur. With reported lengths up to 20 feet, half of that length is in their tails. They use these tails to quickly swim through the water. Watch them from far away though, they can run fast on land too if you're in range.

GREAT BLUE HERON

From the river, we are paddling up Rock Springs Run, where we meet the great blue heron. This is the biggest of the herons that hang out in Florida, standing at 4-foot tall. They can be found all around America, but I've noticed the most in Florida around rivers and other waterways, their principle habitat. These birds are quite patient. They wait for their food to come to them. They will stand in shallow waters waiting for a small reptile, fish or insect to pass by and snatch it up with its long bill.

SOUTHERN LEAPORD FROG

We head back on land to the peninsula of Florida at the Bayard Preserve. This easily missed frog was hanging around the Saint Johns River, probably getting some grub. This pointy head frog likes to hang out in shallow freshwater areas, like rivers and lakes. He may stray from the water to get some shade in the summertime though.

FERAL HOGS

Wild hogs aren't native to Florida, but they sure have made it their home. These baby pigs were a little off the trail in the wildlife preserve. History depicts that the famous early Spanish explorers, Hernando De Soto and Ponce de Leon first brought pigs to Florida in the 1500s. The word "feral" literally describes a wild animal descendant from a domestic one, but some of Florida's pigs were always wild. The male hogs have large upper and lower tusks that rub together to keep them sharp. They travel in groups and if an intruder is spotted, one hog will give the alert grunt, sending the whole group fleeing.

RACCOON

Back in our kayak, something catches our eye. Is that a fox with a mask on? Although they look similar to a fox, Raccoons are most closely related to the bear. They are plantigrade animals, which mean they walk on the entire surface of their feet like bears as well as you and me. You are actually 20 times more likely to find them in a city area than the wild. They go where the food is and find homes anywhere. These two were found in their natural wild environment- fish eating creek, which is a wooded area near water where they catch frogs and other water critters as well as plants and mice. They are rightfully known for being able to open gates, cages, and are capable of picking change from your pocket.

RED CARDINAL

The red cardinal is so hip that 7 states claim it as their official bird as well as a baseball team! These birds do not migrate south for a winter break. It is also actually the males which are the brightest vibrant red color. The females are more of a brown. Like many animal species, the males look more attractive to take a predator's attention away from the female. They are very territorial in the mating season, so much that at times they attack their own reflection. Luckily there were no mirrors on the Ichetucknee River!

BISON

In search of a larger animal, we are back on foot where we run into this wild roaming bison in Payne's Prairie State Park. They also are not originally from Florida, but have roamed here for hundreds of years. The Spanish explorers of the 1700s had brought them there to be raised as cattle. These hefty guys paved many of the paths Native Americans and early explorers followed.

CRACKER HORSE

Like most pigs and cattle, Cracker horses are not native to Florida either, but were brought here about 500 years ago by Ponce de Leon and other Spanish explorers. The word "cracker" refers to the crack of the whips made by the cowboys who worked the cattle. These horses where depended on greatly by the early settlers to help round cattle, which was a primary industry in the early settlement of Florida. As the cattle industry lessened their dependence, many cracker horses ran wild and flourished until the last half century. One of the few places they can still be seen wild is in Payne's Prairie State Park.

LITTLE BLUE HERON

Is that a little blue heron or a blue little heron? This bird spends the first year of its life completely white. Then it makes the dramatic switch to blue. They have less than a month with mom and dad and then they are on their own. They are quite common in Florida's wetlands. This one calls the Alachua sink within Payne's Prairie home.

RED SHOULDERED HAWK

While on the subject of birds, once in the forest road to the Big Cypress Preserve, I was stopped by this Red shouldered hawk. Luckily, he wasn't going to give me a ticket, this guy is just a loud mouth. Red shouldered hawks are usually found higher up in the trees with the owls, but he wanted to make sure that I heard him. They like to live in wet, tree-filled areas where they hunt frogs, snakes, lizards, and smaller furry critters.

RIVER OTTER

These river critters are one of my favorites! I'm so glad we decided to get back in our kayaks and hit Rainbow River State Park! Part of the Wiesel family, otters are mammals that are quite adapt to the water. They are excellent swimmers, and most of all, super fun. They have a good time showing off their aquabatics, but you have to have a quick eye because they are fast and good at hiding. They've been slipping and sliding on land and water for over 5 million years and can hold their breath for 4 minutes!

FLORIDA RIVER COOTER

As we paddle further down the Rainbow River, we meet one of many of Florida's turtles. Florida has several different species of turtles, but this one is a River Cooter. When the sun is up high, these Cooters come up on logs and rocks to relax and dry off after a night in the water. They will often balance on their bellies (or plastron) and stretch out their legs. They have very sharp claws to help them climb and they will often dive back in the water when they spot you in their territory. Sometimes you can look out along the river and see dozens heads popped up keeping an eye on you. Cooters are always watching!

BARRED OWL

As we get out of the kayak to stretch our legs we run into a Barred owl. These owls are often heard, but hard to see. They perch high in the trees and blend in very well in their surroundings. They are most active in the darker hours making them harder to spot. They will eat just about any animal small enough for them to catch including: mice, squirrels, rabbits, bats, mink, birds, fish, frogs, turtles, and insects. They don't bring home doggy bags either; they eat their prey where it was caught. There's less dishes that way!

PLEATED WOODPECKER

He, he,.. he ha, he! Let me introduce you to the real- life woody woodpecker. This is the species of bird the famous cartoon is based. In real life, they are not the menaces you see on TV. They only like pecking at trees. The woodpecker pecks at the trees to uncover ant tunnels and catches them with their tongue and eats them up. Not long ago he was found on the endangered species list but now is happily found on the Rainbow River along with his fellow feathered friends.

CORMORANT

Speaking of feathered friends, you can often find these birds in "the bat pose." They will rest on a tree and hold their wings out to dry. Most water birds' feathers are waterproof, but not the cormorants. They are good at flying, but spend a lot of time in the water in search of food. They will float on top looking for fish to eat. If they see a possible catch, they will dive completely underwater and swim for their meal. Once their belly is full, they will hang themselves out to dry. I often find them sunning themselves out with the turtles.

WOOD DUCK

Our last host of the Rainbow River is this male wood duck, also known as a "Drake." He is one of the most decorative waterfowl around. In the early 1900s, this became a bad thing as hunters sought after them. The colorful wood ducks are the males, while the females are mostly grey, but with similar appearance. Once per year, the ducks shed their feathers and cannot fly for 3-4 weeks. This is one of the reasons they live in watery areas near thick cover and trees. They eat mostly plants and seeds, but their favorite is acorns, etc. that fall into the water. Kind of like how we like to eat our cereal in a bowl of milk rather than dry.

LIMPKIN BIRD

Connected to the Rainbow River is the Withlacoochee River, where we continue our journey. As we round the river bend a loud noise draws our attention to a bird in a low tree limb. Also called the crying bird, the limpkin likes to be heard. In swampy areas, the limpkin will feed on apple snails by striking its beak through the center of the shell and pulling the snail out to munch on. Florida is the only state in North America to house these birds; you'll need a passport to see them anywhere else.

GOLDEN SILK SPIDER

It's time to get out of the kayak and stretch our legs on a hike. As soon as we get a good hiking pace, we run into a sticky web. Known to most native southerners, it's no surprise to be what's commonly called a banana spider, even though I never had one give me a banana. In late summer and fall, the large golden webs of this species make a sticky trap. However, as is typical with most spiders, there is little real danger from an encounter with the golden silk spider. The spider will bite only if held or pinched and you probably won't feel it much.

EASTERN DIAMOND BACK RATTLESNAKE

It was time to get out of the woods and get some sun at Saint George Island State park. Do you know who also likes to get sun? These "rattlers" do, and can be just as dangerous as scary. Just because you don't hear a rattle from his tail, doesn't mean he is not a rattlesnake or won't attack. Rattlesnakes break and lose their rattles from time to time so they can't rattle until it grows back. They are an important part of nature as all animals, but should be appreciated from a distance and not disturbed.

GHOST CRAB

The beach is probably the last place you would look for a ghost, but that's where they all hang out. Of course I'm talking about ghost crabs, sometimes just called sand crabs. They are called ghost crabs because they can hide just like one due to the fact that they camouflage into the sand well and they are out and about mostly at night. The males have one claw that is bigger than the other. And yes this model of crabs comes with airbags! They have sacks by their gills where they store air which they breathe for six weeks during winter hibernation.

WEST INDIAN MANATEE

You can't talk about Florida wildlife without mentioning the manatee. So we're "back in the Paddle" again to meet up with one. Also known as the sea cow, these very large sea creatures are gentle giants. They eat vegetation and are of no threat to humans. They live out in the deep sea but come to Florida during the colder months for its warm springs which remain 70-72 degrees all year round. Manatee can be curious and even playful with humans but approaching them is not allowed. They move very gently and slowly, so much that moss tends to grow on them. Judged by their skeletal structure, it is believed that at one time, long ago, manatees lived on land. Could you imagine walking up to one of these giant teddy bears in your back yard?

SANDHILL CRANE

Is that a heron? No sir'ee, judging by that red spot on the top of its head, it is definitely a sandhill crane. Another clue is they fly with that red head sticking far out while herons fly with their heads tucked back. Some of these cranes spend all their time in Florida, while others migrate from the great lakes in the winter. This Mom and kid team was spotted on the way to Myakka River State Park.

ROSEATE SPOONBILL

These spoonbills are the only type of the pink variety in the
world and they are native to Florida. These particular utensil-
shaped-beak-having birds like to hang out in Myakka River
State Park, near Sarasota, Florida. These birds are also found
in South America, but do not travel much north even in the
warmer months.

RHESUS MONKEY

Monkeys in Florida? Yes. Florida does have wild monkeys, but they are not natural to the area. Years ago, Colonel Tooey operated a Jungle Cruise boat ride along the Silver River near Ocala, Florida. That tour included an island of monkeys he created. Unbeknownst to him, they were able to swim away from their island attraction and have been living along the river for close to 100 years!

WATER SNAKE

This snake must be an old sock. Water snakes generally have stripes, but they darken as they age and the stripes may not be as obvious. You won't find these snakes hanging out on the beach playing volleyball though. They stick to freshwater which includes, fresh rivers, ponds, lakes, streams and marshy swamp areas. We see this one further on down the Silver River which is a freshwater, spring-fed river; complying with the snake's salt-free diet of water. They like to eat fish and other aquatic life, so you won't find them in dry areas.

MISCHIEVOUS GRASSHOPPER

Even as we make a Pit stop home we can find wildlife. This jumpy bug was clinging to a bush in my backyard when I got home. There are many species of grasshoppers living in Florida. This one is assumed to be a "mischievous grasshopper" possibly because of that suspicious look in his eyes. Two major identifiers are the slanting of the face and whether they have long wings or not. They are found in old fields and open woods, and also in my backyard throughout the summer.

FOX SQUIRREL

Is it a fox? Is it a squirrel? By name, it's both. From bug eyes to bushy tale, here is another backyard buddy. The fox squirrel does not have any relation to the fox, just similarities. It has a similar colored coat, a long bushy tail, and trots along similar to a fox so at a distance it can fool anyone. These squirrels are about three times the size of your normal tree squirrel and can be found throughout Florida, but are much rarer than an average tree squirrel. They use those bushy tails for balance and shed their fur twice per year.

WASP

Ouch! Is the first thought that comes to mind when I think of a wasp. You probably have seen a wasp in your neck of the woods, but can you tell the difference between a wasp and a bee? They are not the same. A wasp is skinnier than a bee and is not all fuzzy like a bee is. Also, good to know: A wasp can sting you more than once where a bee cannot. There are over 100,000 species of wasps and I'm sure they all hurt if you get stung, but keep in mind they are part of nature's circle of life. Wasps don't make honey and if you mush one, it releases a smell for other wasps to warn and signal them to retaliate. So it is best to avoid them rather than try to stomp them.

ZEBRA SWALLOWTAIL BUTTERFLY

Has anyone ever asked you if you've seen a Eurytides Marcellus? What did you say? You can likely say yes; it's a fancy name for a Zebra Swallowtail butterfly. When the flowers start blooming in Florida, this only native kite swallowtail can be found feeding. The one pictured here is one of the hundreds stopping for a visit in my backyard. They are easily recognized by the zebra-like stripes on their wings which can reach a span of four inches. Wave goodbye as we set off to out next adventure!

TURKEY VULTURE

As we take a ride through the Cape Canaveral Seashore, we find two suspicious looking birds. It may be scary to see them flying above you during a long hot walk, but Vultures are a part of nature's life cycle. Vultures feed on only dead animals so there is no need to be afraid of them despite their wing span of up to six feet. These massive birds can often hover in the sky without flapping their wings very often as they sniff out their food. They have a much better sense of smell than most birds which tend to rely more on eyesight.

BROWN BAT

Florida is a long way from Transylvania, but it is still batty in spots. We came out of the woods for a break and the wildlife followed us.   Bats aren't very common in Florida but can be found in certain places. These "big brown bats" have a wingspan of 13-14 inches. Naturally they live inside hollow trees, but they find homes in bridges and in purpose-made bat houses as seen in this picture from Gainesville, Florida. Bats feed on insects and hunt at night. Moments after dusk, thousands of bats fly from the house and go out into the night to eat.

DUCK POND DUCK

Florida wildlife can be seen just about anywhere. This duckling was the newest addition to a local duck pond which hatched right by one of my lunchtime picnic tables. This newborn duckling is taking a rest like you would after an exhausting day of hatching. Nature is all around us, but hides well so you have to keep an eye out to catch what's out there.

DRAGONFLY

As we make our way to the Suwannee Wildlife Refuge pier we run into a dragonfly. These are huge bugs and look quite menacing, but they are quite safe and friendly. In prehistoric times these bugs flapped the earth with a wingspan of 28 inches, likely longer than the length of your arm. Baby dragonflies are called nymphs and live underwater. A dragonfly's body may look like a big stinger, but it's not. They have teeth, but they only use them to gnaw on mosquitos. They have big "buggy" eyes that almost touch. If you see a smaller version without as large of eyes, you would be looking at a damselfly.

BALD EAGLE

It's a bird... it's a plane... no, it's a bird; just a very big one. Nothing says America like the American bald eagle, and this one was in the state capital of Tallahassee. They are an endangered species, but I have seen dozens of them in my travels through Florida. In fact, Florida has one of the densest concentrations of nesting eagles in the USA. They tend to nest in areas where wetlands are near. Eagles have excellent eyes and I can vouch for that. They can see another eagle from 50 miles away! You would need super powers to trick an eagle's eye.

THE FOX

This guy has been watching us hike past. Can you guess the biggest difference between a red fox and a grey fox? If you said color, guess again. "Grey" foxes can actually have a lot of red hair too, but red foxes don't have grey hair. The biggest difference is behavioral. The red fox likes to live in fields and pastures where the grey fox likes to hide out in heavily wooded areas. They mostly eat bugs but will also enjoy a variety of fruit, rabbits, and even fish. The grey fox lives in Florida as well as the red fox, but they're the only canine species that are able to climb up a tree.

AMERICAN WHITE IBIS

Continuing in our hiking shoes, this time at Carney Island, we see a white ibis flapping away from us. These birds can be found anywhere in Florida where there is water, which is nearly anywhere in this state. It is said to primarily eat insects and aquatic life, but I have known them to beg for bread with a gang of ducks in a local pond. They don't see well, they rely on probing their beaks to find food. These birds are actually born with a tooth for hatching out of their egg. It falls off in about a week after hatching so you won't find any buck-toothed birds flying around.

WHITE-TAILED DEER

A lot of green grows along this trail, which makes it appealing to the deer. Deer are vegetarians, Eating mostly leaves, twigs, and nuts, which are plentiful here. There are only a few predators deer need to worry about; the panther, bobcats, and the occasional bear. Deer are also the highest hunted animal by humans in Florida, helping contain the species and economy, but leaves less for the panthers to eat. Deer have antlers, which are different than horns. Horns are permanent on an animal. Deer shed their antlers every year near the beginning of spring and regrow them a few months later.

FLORIDA BOBCAT

If you think it is hard finding your pet cat in the house try spotting one of these guys in a vast wooded area. The bobcat gets its name from its short, bobbed tail; unlike your sneaky housecat which has that long skinny tail that has surely knocked a few things over before. Bobcats are primarily meat-eaters. Their top choice for dinner, lunch, breakfast, or anytime is rabbits. When they're feeling spunky, they will eat a bat and even sometimes a deer which is 20 times its size. You won't find a bunch of bobcats hanging out together unless it's the mother with young. They generally live alone and are protective of their territories, some being 25-30 square miles. The mother will raise the baby cats, but within the first year, after being taught how to hunt and survive, they are kicked out on their own and expected to find their own territory likely never to see mother again.

SEA SNAIL

From freshwater to salt water, it's time to hit the beach! When you spot one of these shelled creepy crawlers in the shallow waters of the beach you may yell out that you found a hermit crab. This coruscation is actually a sea snail. Also mistaken as a conch, these creatures can actually drill right through the shell of a crab and eat their meat. Upon finding one they are likely to just hide in their shell until you throw them back in the ocean. This guy came out to say hi and asked directions on how to get back to the water in Naples where he lives.

OSPREY

As we paddle on to Ozello on the west coast we run into quite a big bird who has a keen eye on us. Not much smaller than an eagle, the Osprey is quite impressive in size. Their wingspan is 5-6 feet wide allowing them enough strength to catch and fly away with a pretty good sized fish. They have very powerful claws, or talons which help them catch and grip a fish. Unlike many fish eating birds, Osprey hover high in the air where they spot their prey. Then they swoop down talon-first and grasp a fish right out of the water without diving under. They build stick nests usually high up in a tree or often on radio towers and buoys. They will reuse their nests often for years. After all, wouldn't you after all that work?

ANIMALS WORK TOGETHER JUST LIKE HUMANS, EVEN DIFFERENT SPECIES. THIS MAMA TURTLE CARRIES HER YOUNG JUST LIKE YOUR MOM CARRIED YOU AS A BABY. THE NEXT PHOTO SHOWS IT DOESN'T MATTER WEATHER YOU'RE SHELLED OR FEATHERED, THERE IS ROOM ON THE LOG FOR THE BOTH OF THEM.

LIVING TOGETHER

These two animals would likely run from you if you came near them. Here in Payne's Prairie state park, this wild cracker horse and bison are not threatened by each other. The bison is taking a break from plowing through the watery marsh and isn't threatened by the approaching horse. He knows the horse is just stopping for lunch and won't hurt him. The horse trusts the bison in the same respect. In the wild, humans are considered an intruder to most of the wild. They are very unlikely to attack, but will run not knowing your intentions.

BEFORE YOU RUN OFF…

There is much to be loved and admired by Florida's nature and wildlife. I hope you enjoyed meeting some of the wild of Florida. It is important to know that all the animals help keep the planet in the state it is. It is fun to visit the parks and forests where they live, and as cuddly as they seem, they should not be approached. Feeding them will actually hurt them, so just enjoy spotting them and let them get back to their animal stuff. Just as you would be mad if a bear messed up your room, don't mess up their wilderness.

Leave nothing but footprints…

Works Consulted:

Otter-world.com. Bioexpedition, n.d. Web. 11 Jan 2014.

Defenders.org. Defenders of Wildlife. n.d. Web. 11 Jan 2014.

H.V. Weems, Jr., and G.B. Edwards, "Golden Silk Spider" Jr. Florida department of agriculture and consumer services, August 2001. Web. 15 Jan 2014

Gopher Tortoise Facts. Gopher tortoise facts and gopher tortoise services INC. n.d. Web. 24 Aug 2014

Defenders.org. Defenders of Wildlife. n.d. Web 11 Jan 2014.

(bears)Florida Fish and Wildlife Conservation Commission. *Myfwc.com.* n.d. Web. 15 Jan 2014.

Anirudh. *Ghost Crab (Sand Crab).* Animal Spot. n.d. Web. 28 Jan 2014

Southern Leopard Frog. University of Florida Wildlife Extension. N.d. Web. 15 Jan 2014

Eastern Diamond Back Rattlesnake. National Geographic. n.d, Web 15 Jan 2014

Giuliano, William M. "Wild Hogs in Florida: Ecology and Management" *The University of Florida IFAS extension.* The University of Florida, 2013. Web. 15 Jan 2014

Alderfer, Jonathan. *Complete Birds of North America.* National Geographic. 2006. Web. 31 JAN 2014 (hawk)

Pileated Woodpecker Central. Pileated Woodpecker Central. N.d. Web. 01 FEB 2014

Florida Birds: Owls. Floridian Nature. n.d. Web. 12 DEC 2013

Visit Crystal River Florida & Swim with the Manatee. Swimwiththemanatee.biz. 2013. Web. 15 Jan 2014

The Florida Cracker. Dally Up Ranch. Sep 2011. Web. 23 Jan 2014

Joseph M. Schaefer, Jennifer Cohen, and Mark E. Hostetler. *The Wood Duck.* The University of Florida IFAS extension. 2013. Web. 05 Jan 2014

Cardinal. National Geograpic. National Georgraphic. n.d. Web. 12 Dec 2013.

Heintz, D.C. *Cormorant.* Night Breeze. 2010. Web. 02 Jan 2014

Florida Nature: Squirrels. Floridian Nature. n.d. Web 05 Feb 2014

Little Blue Heron. All About Birds. The Cornell Lab of Orthinology. n.d. Web. 16 Jan 2014

Sandhill Crane: Grus Canadensis. Myfwc.com. Florida Fish and Wildlife Conservation Commission. n.d. Web. 15 Dec 2013

Works consulted (con't):

Mayntz,Melissa. *About Birding.* About.com. n.d. Web. 02 Feb 2014 (spoonbill)

Lad, Kashmira. *Interesting Facts About Bottlenose Dolphins.* Buzzle.com. May 2013. Web. 01 Jan 2014

Wildlife facts #389: Do they have Bananas in Space? Wildfacts.com. n.d, Web. 01 Feb 2014

Grasshoppers of Florida. Universiy of Florida Food and Agricultural Services. N.d. Web. 15 Jan 2014

Florida Butterflies. Floridasnature.com. n.d. Web 28 Jan 2014

Florida Birds: Vultures. Floridian Nature. n.d. Web. 15 Jan 2014

Florida Scrub Jay. Florida Fish and Wildlife service. N.d. Web. 01 Mar 2014

The Florida Bat Conservatory. 2005 Web. 05 FEB 2014.

"Limpkin" *Encyclopedia Britannica Online.* Encyclopedia Britannica, n.d. Web. 05 Feb 2014.

"Dragonflies." Holoweb.com. Minnesota Holoweb. N.d. Web. 05 FEB 2014

"Florida Birds: American Eagle and Osprey." *Floridian Nature.* Floridian Nature. n.d. Web. 05 FEB 2014

"Great Blue Heron - *Ardea herodias*" *Nature Works.* Nature Works. 2014. Web. 28 Jan 2014

"American White Ibis." *Wikipedia.* Wikimedia. N.d. Web. 25 Jan 20014

"Fun Facts About Wasps." *Interesting Fun Facts.* Interesting Fun Facts. N.d. Web. 20 Jan 2014

"Floridian Nature: Florida Deer." *Floridian Nature.* Discover Florida Nature. n.d. Web. 20 Jan 2014

"Florida Nature: Red Fox and Gray Fox." *Floridian Nature.* Discover Florida Nature. n.d. Web. 20 Jan 2014

"Basic Facts About Bobcats." *Defenders of Wildlife.* Defenders of Wildlife. n.d. Web. 18 Jan 2014

"Dusky Pigmy Rattlesnake." *Seworld Wildlife.* Seaworld Wildlife Organization. N.d. Web. 15 Jan 2014

"Big Cypress Fox Squirrel." *Dicke Brewer .org.* Dick Brewer Organiztion. N.d. Web. 15 Jan 2014

"Raccoon." *The Jungle Store.* The Jungle Store. N.d Web. 15 Jan 2014

Buchsbaum, M.Ra.P., Vicki & John. *Living Invertebrates.* 1987. Web. Pacific Grove, CA. The Boxwood Press. 15 Jan 2014

"Florida Cooter." *Wikipedia."* Wikimedia. N.d. Web. 15